From
BURNOUT
to
BALANCE

A Nursing Resilience Journal

ANGELA L. HOSKING, RN

ORANGE BLOSSOM
PUBLISHING

Maitland, Florida

This Journal Belongs to

....

Published 2021 by Orange Blossom Publishing
Maitland, Florida
www.orangeblossombooks.com
info@orangeblossombooks.com

ISBN: 978-1-949935-24-0

"I never lose an opportunity of urging a practical beginning, however small, for it is wonderful how often in such matters the mustard-seed germinates and roots itself."

– Florence Nightingale

Dedication

This journal is dedicated to every nurse who has found their way by being lost in the service of others. Self-compassion is often the hardest gift we can give to ourselves, so as your nurse I am prescribing it for you. When pinned, we all participated in the Lamp Lighting ceremony in honor of Florence Nightingale. It was her lamp that became the symbol of the light and enlightenment that comes with our nursing knowledge. An empty lantern can provide no light. It is time to refuel yours.

Angela Hosking, MBA MSN RN NE-BC

Introduction

I remember my first patient that died.

She was young. Younger than me. A mom, a daughter, a sister, and a passionate elementary school teacher. She was living her life in a happy and fulfilling way when ovarian cancer knocked on her door. When I cared for her the first time, she was recovering from a dramatic abdominal surgery and coming to grips with the diagnosis. Stage 4 ovarian cancer. We focused on her post-operative recovery for the first few days, but as the diagnosis began to sink in, I found our conversations turned to how to be a survivor and have hope. I became her cheerleader, her confidant, and when her family went home, her advocate as a nursing professional.

I saw her when she was the most vulnerable. In pain. Frightened. As a night-shift nurse, I was used to the "what-if" thoughts that plagued my patients in the night when the comfort of the family departed. That is when they usually allowed their nurse to see what they were really feeling. When faces of feigned bravery for their families could relax.

Over the next eighteen months, I was lucky enough to care for her many times. Even if she wasn't my patient for that shift, I made sure to check on her every time she was admitted for symptom management or pain control. I learned what worked and what didn't when she was having a bad night. I knew the right mix of bland food she could tolerate when the nausea was bad. I helped her make a list of all the things she wanted to remember to tell her daughter when her mind was fuzzy. Sometimes I even made her laugh with my corny jokes and just forget for a moment that she was dying.

When she lost her battle, I was there. I made sure she wasn't in any pain, that her favorite blanket was tucked around her just so, and that her family was supported. But what I didn't realize was that I would need support, too. I was grieving a loss that had a monumental impact on how I viewed my role as a nursing caregiver. I was now acutely aware that many of the patients I bonded with would die on my watch.

Over and over again.

And to give in such an extraordinary way, I would have to make sure I was being cared for as well. I had to allow others to calm my fears, dry my tears, and give space for the emotions I had at work. I was not, thankfully, a machine instead of a human that just went about her nightshift as if nothing happened.

To be a nurse means to first care for ourselves so that we can care for others. This journal was created for you to process your feelings, lighten your burden, and move from burnout to balance.

You are your most vulnerable patient. Take time to do your assessment carefully.

Angela L. Hosking, RN

My Current State

When was the last time you did a complete head-to-toe on yourself? A mental, physical, and emotional check-up to see what systems and areas are NOT within normal limits? It is easy to deny that nagging inner-nurse voice when it comes to ourselves. But if you were your patient, what would you tell the provider you were concerned about? What recommendations would you make for your own care? What consults would you immediately advocate for?

So, like any focused assessment, we are going to start with your chief complaints.

□────────────────□

1) What brought you to this journal? What's bothering you most right now? Report any areas of concern related to your overall physical health, emotional health, and spiritual health. If we could prescribe an imaginary treatment or medication regimen, what problem(s) would it solve for you?

....
....
....
....
....
....
....
....

2) What fundamental well-being practices have you been neglecting, and why? Sleep? Nutrition? Exercise? Breaks?

....
....
....
....
....
....
....

3) What unhealthy coping mechanisms have you been using to deal with stress? Which ones do you want to stop or reduce?

....

....

....

....

....

....

....

....

....

4) On a scale of 1-10, what is your daily level of personal stress, feelings of burnout or depersonalization, or readiness to quit your profession?

1 = well balanced
5 = somewhat balanced but it needs tweaking
10 = danger zone, I feel unbalanced and unwell

5) What has worked well for you in the past related to stress management and strengthening your resilience to come back from a hard day?

....

....

....

....

....

....

....

....

....

6) What is not going well at work? What are safety, support, or morale concerns that need to be brought to the attention of your leader? What could you be doing to help advocate for a healthier work environment?

....
....
....
....
....
....
....
....

7) Identify two goals, one physical and one mental, that you will work towards during this journaling process. Make it specific, measurable, attainable within a timeframe, relevant to the needs you identified above, and timebound. An example: I will take my full 30-minute lunch break to rest and refuel and will not work through lunch for the next 30 days.

Goal Number One: (physical)

....
....
....

Goal Number Two: (mental)

....
....
....

What new habit would you like to create as it relates to both?

....
....
....

Quotes To Live By

"Caring is the essence of nursing." -Jean Watson

"I have learned to live each day as it comes and not to borrow trouble by dreading tomorrow." -Dorothea Dix

"Nurses are a unique kind. They have an insatiable need to care for others which is both their greatest strength and fatal flaw."- Jean Watson

"When you're a nurse, you know that every day you will touch a life or a life will touch yours." -Unknown

"When I think about all the patients and their loved ones that I have worked with over the years, I know most of them don't remember me nor I to them, but I do know that I gave a little piece of myself to each of them and they to me and those threads make up the beautiful tapestry in my mind that is my career in nursing." -Donna Wilk Cardillo

"The challenge is not to be perfect—it's to be whole." -Jane Fonda

"You yourself, as much as anybody in the entire universe, deserve your love and affection." -Budda

"Love yourself enough to set boundaries." -Anna Taylor

"As you grow older, you will discover that you have two hands, one for helping yourself, the other for helping others." -Maya Angelou

Add your favorite(s):

....

....

....

....

....

Nursing Mantras

When I feel overwhelmed by my patient assignment, I will tell myself

....

....

....

....

....

When I have a patient that challenges my patience, I will tell myself

....

....

....

....

....

When I need help, but I don't want to ask, I will tell myself

....

....

....

....

....

When a patient has an outcome that leaves me feeling defeated, I will tell myself

....

....

....

....

When I am tired, and question my career choice, I will tell myself

....

....

....

....

From Burnout to Balance:
The Nursing Resilience Focus Journal Method

This journal is designed to be your weekly partner to help you have a plan to manage stress and anxiety, and mitigate the emotional and physical drain from long nursing shifts. Each week you will spend 10 minutes creating your plan at the beginning of the week, and 10 minutes reflecting at the end of the week so you can see learnings, make progress, and find balance between your work and the rest of your life. Each month there is a longer journal prompt for you to dive deeper into your thoughts and feelings as you practice balance, strengthen your resiliency muscle, and care for yourself in the way you care for others. There is no right or wrong way to use this journal. Make it yours.

Set a Schedule for Journaling

When I will complete the Planning page each week:

Day of the week: .... Time of day: ....

When I will complete the Reflections page each week:

Day of the week: .... Time of day: ....

How will you remind yourself to fill in your focus journal?

....

....

....

WEEK 1

Planning

My physical goal focus for this week

My emotional goal focus for this week

My anxious thoughts are

What's causing my anxiety?

I will care for myself at work this week by

One way I will manage fatigue this week

Something I will do just for me this week

I will schedule fun this week by

WEEK 1

Reflections

One thing that challenged me this week

What I learned from the challenge

A thought I need to let go of is

I will practice doing this by

I was proud of myself this week for

A moment at work that connected me back to my purpose was

How balanced did I feel this week (1-5)?

One balance tactic I'll do more next week

WEEK 2

Planning

My physical goal focus for this week

My emotional goal focus for this week

My anxious thoughts are

What's causing my anxiety?

I will care for myself at work this week by

One way I will manage fatigue this week

Something I will do just for me this week

I will schedule fun this week by

WEEK 2

Reflections

One thing that challenged me this week

What I learned from the challenge

A thought I need to let go of is

I will practice doing this by

I was proud of myself this week for

A moment at work that connected me back to my purpose was

How balanced did I feel this week (1-5)?

One balance tactic I'll do more next week

WEEK 3

Planning

My physical goal focus for this week

My emotional goal focus for this week

My anxious thoughts are

What's causing my anxiety?

I will care for myself at work this week by

One way I will manage fatigue this week

Something I will do just for me this week

I will schedule fun this week by

WEEK 3

Reflections

One thing that challenged me this week

What I learned from the challenge

A thought I need to let go of is

I will practice doing this by

I was proud of myself this week for

A moment at work that connected me back to my purpose was

How balanced did I feel this week (1-5)?

One balance tactic I'll do more next week

WEEK 4

Planning

I will care for myself at work this week by

My physical goal focus for this week

One way I will manage fatigue this week

My emotional goal focus for this week

Something I will do just for me this week

My anxious thoughts are

I will schedule fun this week by

What's causing my anxiety?

WEEK 4

Reflections

One thing that challenged me this week

What I learned from the challenge

A thought I need to let go of is

I will practice doing this by

I was proud of myself this week for

A moment at work that connected me back to my purpose was

How balanced did I feel this week (1-5)?

One balance tactic I'll do more next week

MONTHLY REFLECTION

What went well this month? What lessons did I apply from the focus journal that made me feel more balanced?

....
....
....
....

What was difficult? Where do I need to adjust either my physical goal or mental goal to be more balanced?

....
....
....
....

What is working well in my work environment? Do I need to adjust the way my shifts are scheduled? Is it time for me to schedule time off for the next month?

....
....
....
....

What would make me feel more supported and balanced at work? How could I suggest this change to my leadership team? My teammates?

....
....
....
....

How is my resilience growing? What experience did I bounce back from that made me proud?

....
....
....
....

One thing I will schedule just for me next month is

....
....

Reconnect With Your Why

Reflect on your "why" for becoming a nurse. What drew you into the profession and what were you excited about when embarking on this new career? What could you put "more of" into your daily work that rekindles this why?

....

....

....

....

....

....

....

....

....

....

....

....

....

....

....

....

....

....

....

....

....

....

....

....

....

WEEK 5

Planning

My physical goal focus for this week

My emotional goal focus for this week

My anxious thoughts are

What's causing my anxiety?

I will care for myself at work this week by

One way I will manage fatigue this week

Something I will do just for me this week

I will schedule fun this week by

WEEK 5

Reflections

One thing that challenged me this week

What I learned from the challenge

A thought I need to let go of is

I will practice doing this by

I was proud of myself this week for

A moment at work that connected me back to my purpose was

How balanced did I feel this week (1-5)?

One balance tactic I'll do more next week

WEEK 6

Planning

My physical goal focus for this week

My emotional goal focus for this week

My anxious thoughts are

What's causing my anxiety?

I will care for myself at work this week by

One way I will manage fatigue this week

Something I will do just for me this week

I will schedule fun this week by

WEEK 6

Reflections

One thing that challenged me this week

What I learned from the challenge

A thought I need to let go of is

I will practice doing this by

I was proud of myself this week for

A moment at work that connected me back to my purpose was

How balanced did I feel this week (1-5)?

One balance tactic I'll do more next week

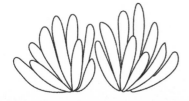

WEEK 7

Planning

I will care for myself at work this week by

My physical goal focus for this week

One way I will manage fatigue this week

My emotional goal focus for this week

Something I will do just for me this week

My anxious thoughts are

I will schedule fun this week by

What's causing my anxiety?

WEEK 7

Reflections

One thing that challenged me this week

What I learned from the challenge

A thought I need to let go of is

I will practice doing this by

I was proud of myself this week for

A moment at work that connected me back to my purpose was

How balanced did I feel this week (1-5)?

One balance tactic I'll do more next week

WEEK 8

Planning

I will care for myself at work this week by

My physical goal focus for this week

One way I will manage fatigue this week

My emotional goal focus for this week

Something I will do just for me this week

My anxious thoughts are

I will schedule fun this week by

What's causing my anxiety?

WEEK 8

Reflections

One thing that challenged me this week

What I learned from the challenge

A thought I need to let go of is

I will practice doing this by

I was proud of myself this week for

A moment at work that connected me back to my purpose was

How balanced did I feel this week (1-5)?

One balance tactic I'll do more next week

MONTHLY REFLECTION

What went well this month? What lessons did I apply from the focus journal that made me feel more balanced?

....
....
....
....

What was difficult? Where do I need to adjust either my physical goal or mental goal to be more balanced?

....
....
....
....

What is working well in my work environment? Do I need to adjust the way my shifts are scheduled? Is it time for me to schedule time off for the next month?

....
....
....
....

What would make me feel more supported and balanced at work? How could I suggest this change to my leadership team? My teammates?

....
....
....
....

How is my resilience growing? What experience did I bounce back from that made me proud?

....
....
....
....

One thing I will schedule just for me next month is

....
....

A Letter to a "Friend"

Nurses are often hard on themselves when they feel they didn't give their patients enough time to truly listen to their concerns. Perhaps you recently had a day where you felt rushed, pressured, or had a patient that needed more attention than others. Give yourself grace and write a reflection that helps you let go of any feelings of inadequacy or perfectionistic thoughts. Talk to yourself as if you were comforting a peer feeling this way.

WEEK 9

Planning

My physical goal focus for this week

I will care for myself at work this week by

My emotional goal focus for this week

One way I will manage fatigue this week

My anxious thoughts are

Something I will do just for me this week

What's causing my anxiety?

I will schedule fun this week by

WEEK 9

Reflections

One thing that challenged me this week

What I learned from the challenge

A thought I need to let go of is

I will practice doing this by

I was proud of myself this week for

A moment at work that connected me back to my purpose was

How balanced did I feel this week (1-5)?

One balance tactic I'll do more next week

WEEK 10

Planning

My physical goal focus for this week

I will care for myself at work this week by

My emotional goal focus for this week

One way I will manage fatigue this week

My anxious thoughts are

Something I will do just for me this week

What's causing my anxiety?

I will schedule fun this week by

WEEK 10

Reflections

One thing that challenged me this week

What I learned from the challenge

A thought I need to let go of is

I will practice doing this by

I was proud of myself this week for

A moment at work that connected me back to my purpose was

How balanced did I feel this week (1-5)?

One balance tactic I'll do more next week

WEEK 11

Planning

My physical goal focus for this week

I will care for myself at work this week by

My emotional goal focus for this week

One way I will manage fatigue this week

My anxious thoughts are

Something I will do just for me this week

What's causing my anxiety?

I will schedule fun this week by

WEEK 11

Reflections

One thing that challenged me this week

What I learned from the challenge

A thought I need to let go of is

I will practice doing this by

I was proud of myself this week for

A moment at work that connected me back to my purpose was

How balanced did I feel this week (1-5)?

One balance tactic I'll do more next week

WEEK 12

Planning

My physical goal focus for this week

I will care for myself at work this week by

My emotional goal focus for this week

One way I will manage fatigue this week

My anxious thoughts are

Something I will do just for me this week

What's causing my anxiety?

I will schedule fun this week by

WEEK 12

Reflections

One thing that challenged me this week

What I learned from the challenge

A thought I need to let go of is

I will practice doing this by

I was proud of myself this week for

A moment at work that connected me back to my purpose was

How balanced did I feel this week (1-5)?

One balance tactic I'll do more next week

MONTHLY REFLECTION

What went well this month? What lessons did I apply from the focus journal that made me feel more balanced?

....

....

....

....

What was difficult? Where do I need to adjust either my physical goal or mental goal to be more balanced?

....

....

....

....

What is working well in my work environment? Do I need to adjust the way my shifts are scheduled? Is it time for me to schedule time off for the next month?

....

....

....

....

What would make me feel more supported and balanced at work? How could I suggest this change to my leadership team? My teammates?

....

....

....

....

How is my resilience growing? What experience did I bounce back from that made me proud?

....

....

....

....

One thing I will schedule just for me next month is

....

....

Recentering Focus Mantras

Setting an intention prior to a shift can help you to feel more grounded and stay in a "self-care" mindset when having a rough day. Think of this as a mental mantra to come back to when stressors are present. Craft three intentional statements that you can use this next week that will re-center you.

....
....
....
....
....
....
....
....
....
....
....
....
....
....
....
....
....
....
....
....
....
....
....
....
....
....
....

WEEK 13

Planning

My physical goal focus for this week

My emotional goal focus for this week

My anxious thoughts are

What's causing my anxiety?

I will care for myself at work this week by

One way I will manage fatigue this week

Something I will do just for me this week

I will schedule fun this week by

WEEK 13

Reflections

One thing that challenged me this week

What I learned from the challenge

A thought I need to let go of is

I will practice doing this by

I was proud of myself this week for

A moment at work that connected me back to my purpose was

How balanced did I feel this week (1-5)?

One balance tactic I'll do more next week

WEEK 14

Planning

My physical goal focus for this week

My emotional goal focus for this week

My anxious thoughts are

What's causing my anxiety?

I will care for myself at work this week by

One way I will manage fatigue this week

Something I will do just for me this week

I will schedule fun this week by

WEEK 14

Reflections

One thing that challenged me this week

What I learned from the challenge

A thought I need to let go of is

I will practice doing this by

I was proud of myself this week for

A moment at work that connected me back to my purpose was

How balanced did I feel this week (1-5)?

One balance tactic I'll do more next week

WEEK 15

Planning

I will care for myself at work this week by

My physical goal focus for this week

One way I will manage fatigue this week

My emotional goal focus for this week

Something I will do just for me this week

My anxious thoughts are

I will schedule fun this week by

What's causing my anxiety?

WEEK 15

Reflections

One thing that challenged me this week

What I learned from the challenge

A thought I need to let go of is

I will practice doing this by

I was proud of myself this week for

A moment at work that connected me back to my purpose was

How balanced did I feel this week (1-5)?

One balance tactic I'll do more next week

WEEK 16

Planning

My physical goal focus for this week

My emotional goal focus for this week

My anxious thoughts are

What's causing my anxiety?

I will care for myself at work this week by

One way I will manage fatigue this week

Something I will do just for me this week

I will schedule fun this week by

WEEK 16

Reflections

One thing that challenged me this week

What I learned from the challenge

A thought I need to let go of is

I will practice doing this by

I was proud of myself this week for

A moment at work that connected me back to my purpose was

How balanced did I feel this week (1-5)?

One balance tactic I'll do more next week

MONTHLY REFLECTION

What went well this month? What lessons did I apply from the focus journal that made me feel more balanced?

....

....

....

....

What was difficult? Where do I need to adjust either my physical goal or mental goal to be more balanced?

....

....

....

....

What is working well in my work environment? Do I need to adjust the way my shifts are scheduled? Is it time for me to schedule time off for the next month?

....

....

....

....

What would make me feel more supported and balanced at work? How could I suggest this change to my leadership team? My teammates?

....

....

....

....

How is my resilience growing? What experience did I bounce back from that made me proud?

....

....

....

....

One thing I will schedule just for me next month is

....

....

Focusing on Laughter

Take some time this month to remember occasions where you laughed in your
work day. Perhaps a coworker made a joke, something malfunctioned in a silly way,
or a patient surprised you in a fun way. Jot down the laughs you had this month to see
how many times you smile during your shifts.

....

....

....

....

....

....

....

....

....

....

....

....

....

....

....

....

....

....

....

....

....

....

....

....

WEEK 17

Planning

I will care for myself at work this week by

My physical goal focus for this week

One way I will manage fatigue this week

My emotional goal focus for this week

Something I will do just for me this week

My anxious thoughts are

I will schedule fun this week by

What's causing my anxiety?

WEEK 17

Reflections

One thing that challenged me this week

What I learned from the challenge

A thought I need to let go of is

I will practice doing this by

I was proud of myself this week for

A moment at work that connected me back to my purpose was

How balanced did I feel this week (1-5)?

One balance tactic I'll do more next week

WEEK 18

Planning

My physical goal focus for this week

I will care for myself at work this week by

My emotional goal focus for this week

One way I will manage fatigue this week

My anxious thoughts are

Something I will do just for me this week

What's causing my anxiety?

I will schedule fun this week by

WEEK 18

Reflections

One thing that challenged me this week

What I learned from the challenge

A thought I need to let go of is

I will practice doing this by

I was proud of myself this week for

A moment at work that connected me back to my purpose was

How balanced did I feel this week (1-5)?

One balance tactic I'll do more next week

WEEK 19

Planning

My physical goal focus for this week

My emotional goal focus for this week

My anxious thoughts are

What's causing my anxiety?

I will care for myself at work this week by

One way I will manage fatigue this week

Something I will do just for me this week

I will schedule fun this week by

WEEK 19

Reflections

One thing that challenged me this week

What I learned from the challenge

A thought I need to let go of is

I will practice doing this by

I was proud of myself this week for

A moment at work that connected me back to my purpose was

How balanced did I feel this week (1-5)?

One balance tactic I'll do more next week

WEEK 20

Planning

My physical goal focus for this week

I will care for myself at work this week by

One way I will manage fatigue this week

My emotional goal focus for this week

Something I will do just for me this week

My anxious thoughts are

I will schedule fun this week by

What's causing my anxiety?

WEEK 20

Reflections

One thing that challenged me this week

What I learned from the challenge

A thought I need to let go of is

I will practice doing this by

I was proud of myself this week for

A moment at work that connected me back to my purpose was

How balanced did I feel this week (1-5)?

One balance tactic I'll do more next week

MONTHLY REFLECTION

What went well this month? What lessons did I apply from the focus journal that made me feel more balanced?

....

....

....

....

What was difficult? Where do I need to adjust either my physical goal or mental goal to be more balanced?

....

....

....

....

What is working well in my work environment? Do I need to adjust the way my shifts are scheduled? Is it time for me to schedule time off for the next month?

....

....

....

....

What would make me feel more supported and balanced at work? How could I suggest this change to my leadership team? My teammates?

....

....

....

....

How is my resilience growing? What experience did I bounce back from that made me proud?

....

....

....

....

One thing I will schedule just for me next month is

....

....

Seeing External and Internal

Reflect on a recent day where you felt overwhelmed during a shift. What external forces contributed to you feeling this way? What internal thoughts or beliefs? Reflect on any thoughts that didn't serve you. Ask yourself, what thoughts will I embrace when an overwhelming situation occurs again?

....
....
....
....
....
....
....
....
....
....
....
....
....
....
....
....
....
....
....
....
....
....
....
....
....
....
....

WEEK 21

Planning

My physical goal focus for this week

My emotional goal focus for this week

My anxious thoughts are

What's causing my anxiety?

I will care for myself at work this week by

One way I will manage fatigue this week

Something I will do just for me this week

I will schedule fun this week by

WEEK 21

Reflections

One thing that challenged me this week

What I learned from the challenge

A thought I need to let go of is

I will practice doing this by

I was proud of myself this week for

A moment at work that connected me back to my purpose was

How balanced did I feel this week (1-5)?

One balance tactic I'll do more next week

WEEK 22

Planning

My physical goal focus for this week

My emotional goal focus for this week

My anxious thoughts are

What's causing my anxiety?

I will care for myself at work this week by

One way I will manage fatigue this week

Something I will do just for me this week

I will schedule fun this week by

WEEK 22

Reflections

One thing that challenged me this week

What I learned from the challenge

A thought I need to let go of is

I will practice doing this by

I was proud of myself this week for

A moment at work that connected me back to my purpose was

How balanced did I feel this week (1-5)?

One balance tactic I'll do more next week

WEEK 23

Planning

My physical goal focus for this week

I will care for myself at work this week by

My emotional goal focus for this week

One way I will manage fatigue this week

My anxious thoughts are

Something I will do just for me this week

What's causing my anxiety?

I will schedule fun this week by

WEEK 23

Reflections

One thing that challenged me this week

What I learned from the challenge

A thought I need to let go of is

I will practice doing this by

I was proud of myself this week for

A moment at work that connected me back to my purpose was

How balanced did I feel this week (1-5)?

One balance tactic I'll do more next week

WEEK 24

Planning

My physical goal focus for this week

My emotional goal focus for this week

My anxious thoughts are

What's causing my anxiety?

I will care for myself at work this week by

One way I will manage fatigue this week

Something I will do just for me this week

I will schedule fun this week by

WEEK 24

Reflections

One thing that challenged me this week

What I learned from the challenge

A thought I need to let go of is

I will practice doing this by

I was proud of myself this week for

A moment at work that connected me back to my purpose was

How balanced did I feel this week (1-5)?

One balance tactic I'll do more next week

MONTHLY REFLECTION

What went well this month? What lessons did I apply from the focus journal that made me feel more balanced?

....

....

....

....

What was difficult? Where do I need to adjust either my physical goal or mental goal to be more balanced?

....

....

....

....

What is working well in my work environment? Do I need to adjust the way my shifts are scheduled? Is it time for me to schedule time off for the next month?

....

....

....

....

What would make me feel more supported and balanced at work? How could I suggest this change to my leadership team? My teammates?

....

....

....

....

How is my resilience growing? What experience did I bounce back from that made me proud?

....

....

....

....

One thing I will schedule just for me next month is

....

....

Giving Yourself a Time Out

What physical signs do you notice prior to feeling tense or pressured during
your workday? How could you incorporate a "time out" for yourself when you notice
those sensations? What has been helpful in the past?

....
....
....
....
....
....
....
....
....
....
....
....
....
....
....
....
....
....
....
....
....
....
....
....
....
....

WEEK 25

Planning

My physical goal focus for this week

I will care for myself at work this week by

My emotional goal focus for this week

One way I will manage fatigue this week

My anxious thoughts are

Something I will do just for me this week

What's causing my anxiety?

I will schedule fun this week by

WEEK 25

Reflections

One thing that challenged me this week

What I learned from the challenge

A thought I need to let go of is

I will practice doing this by

I was proud of myself this week for

A moment at work that connected me back to my purpose was

How balanced did I feel this week (1-5)?

One balance tactic I'll do more next week

WEEK 26

Planning

My physical goal focus for this week

I will care for myself at work this week by

My emotional goal focus for this week

One way I will manage fatigue this week

My anxious thoughts are

Something I will do just for me this week

What's causing my anxiety?

I will schedule fun this week by

WEEK 26

Reflections

One thing that challenged me this week

What I learned from the challenge

A thought I need to let go of is

I will practice doing this by

I was proud of myself this week for

A moment at work that connected me back to my purpose was

How balanced did I feel this week (1-5)?

One balance tactic I'll do more next week

WEEK 27

Planning

My physical goal focus for this week

I will care for myself at work this week by

My emotional goal focus for this week

One way I will manage fatigue this week

My anxious thoughts are

Something I will do just for me this week

What's causing my anxiety?

I will schedule fun this week by

WEEK 27

Reflections

One thing that challenged me this week

What I learned from the challenge

A thought I need to let go of is

I will practice doing this by

I was proud of myself this week for

A moment at work that connected me back to my purpose was

How balanced did I feel this week (1-5)?

One balance tactic I'll do more next week

WEEK 28

Planning

My physical goal focus for this week

I will care for myself at work this week by

My emotional goal focus for this week

One way I will manage fatigue this week

My anxious thoughts are

Something I will do just for me this week

What's causing my anxiety?

I will schedule fun this week by

WEEK 28

Reflections

One thing that challenged me this week

What I learned from the challenge

A thought I need to let go of is

I will practice doing this by

I was proud of myself this week for

A moment at work that connected me back to my purpose was

How balanced did I feel this week (1-5)?

One balance tactic I'll do more next week

MONTHLY REFLECTION

What went well this month? What lessons did I apply from the focus journal that made me feel more balanced?

....

....

....

....

What was difficult? Where do I need to adjust either my physical goal or mental goal to be more balanced?

....

....

....

....

What is working well in my work environment? Do I need to adjust the way my shifts are scheduled? Is it time for me to schedule time off for the next month?

....

....

....

....

What would make me feel more supported and balanced at work? How could I suggest this change to my leadership team? My teammates?

....

....

....

....

How is my resilience growing? What experience did I bounce back from that made me proud?

....

....

....

....

One thing I will schedule just for me next month is

....

....

Reflecting on Favorites

What is your favorite part of your workday? When was the last time you had a "good" day? Reflect on what contributed to this fulfilling day.

....
....
....
....
....
....
....
....
....
....
....
....
....
....
....
....
....
....
....
....
....
....
....
....
....
....
....
....
....

WEEK 29

Planning

My physical goal focus for this week

I will care for myself at work this week by

My emotional goal focus for this week

One way I will manage fatigue this week

My anxious thoughts are

Something I will do just for me this week

What's causing my anxiety?

I will schedule fun this week by

WEEK 29

Reflections

One thing that challenged me this week

What I learned from the challenge

A thought I need to let go of is

I will practice doing this by

I was proud of myself this week for

A moment at work that connected me back to my purpose was

How balanced did I feel this week (1-5)?

One balance tactic I'll do more next week

WEEK 30

Planning

My physical goal focus for this week

My emotional goal focus for this week

My anxious thoughts are

What's causing my anxiety?

I will care for myself at work this week by

One way I will manage fatigue this week

Something I will do just for me this week

I will schedule fun this week by

WEEK 30

Reflections

One thing that challenged me this week

What I learned from the challenge

A thought I need to let go of is

I will practice doing this by

I was proud of myself this week for

A moment at work that connected me back to my purpose was

How balanced did I feel this week (1-5)?

One balance tactic I'll do more next week

WEEK 31

Planning

My physical goal focus for this week

I will care for myself at work this week by

My emotional goal focus for this week

One way I will manage fatigue this week

My anxious thoughts are

Something I will do just for me this week

What's causing my anxiety?

I will schedule fun this week by

WEEK 31

Reflections

One thing that challenged me this week

What I learned from the challenge

A thought I need to let go of is

I will practice doing this by

I was proud of myself this week for

A moment at work that connected me back to my purpose was

How balanced did I feel this week (1-5)?

One balance tactic I'll do more next week

WEEK 32

Planning

My physical goal focus for this week

My emotional goal focus for this week

My anxious thoughts are

What's causing my anxiety?

I will care for myself at work this week by

One way I will manage fatigue this week

Something I will do just for me this week

I will schedule fun this week by

WEEK 32

Reflections

One thing that challenged me this week

What I learned from the challenge

A thought I need to let go of is

I will practice doing this by

I was proud of myself this week for

A moment at work that connected me back to my purpose was

How balanced did I feel this week (1-5)?

One balance tactic I'll do more next week

MONTHLY REFLECTION

What went well this month? What lessons did I apply from the focus journal that made me feel more balanced?

....

....

....

....

What was difficult? Where do I need to adjust either my physical goal or mental goal to be more balanced?

....

....

....

....

What is working well in my work environment? Do I need to adjust the way my shifts are scheduled? Is it time for me to schedule time off for the next month?

....

....

....

....

What would make me feel more supported and balanced at work? How could I suggest this change to my leadership team? My teammates?

....

....

....

....

How is my resilience growing? What experience did I bounce back from that made me proud?

....

....

....

....

One thing I will schedule just for me next month is

....

....

Examing Thought Patterns

In what ways do you self-sabotage and deplete yourself mentally or physically? Why do you think this reoccurs? When have you been successful in circumventing this self-sabotage?

....
....
....
....
....
....
....
....
....
....
....
....
....
....
....
....
....
....
....
....
....
....
....
....
....

WEEK 33

Planning

My physical goal focus for this week

My emotional goal focus for this week

My anxious thoughts are

What's causing my anxiety?

I will care for myself at work this week by

One way I will manage fatigue this week

Something I will do just for me this week

I will schedule fun this week by

WEEK 33

Reflections

One thing that challenged me this week

What I learned from the challenge

A thought I need to let go of is

I will practice doing this by

I was proud of myself this week for

A moment at work that connected me back to my purpose was

How balanced did I feel this week (1-5)?

One balance tactic I'll do more next week

WEEK 34

Planning

My physical goal focus for this week

I will care for myself at work this week by

My emotional goal focus for this week

One way I will manage fatigue this week

My anxious thoughts are

Something I will do just for me this week

What's causing my anxiety?

I will schedule fun this week by

WEEK 34

Reflections

One thing that challenged me this week

What I learned from the challenge

A thought I need to let go of is

I will practice doing this by

I was proud of myself this week for

A moment at work that connected me back to my purpose was

How balanced did I feel this week (1-5)?

One balance tactic I'll do more next week

WEEK 35

Planning

My physical goal focus for this week

I will care for myself at work this week by

My emotional goal focus for this week

One way I will manage fatigue this week

My anxious thoughts are

Something I will do just for me this week

What's causing my anxiety?

I will schedule fun this week by

WEEK 35

Reflections

One thing that challenged me this week

What I learned from the challenge

A thought I need to let go of is

I will practice doing this by

I was proud of myself this week for

A moment at work that connected me back to my purpose was

How balanced did I feel this week (1-5)?

One balance tactic I'll do more next week

WEEK 36

Planning

My physical goal focus for this week

I will care for myself at work this week by

My emotional goal focus for this week

One way I will manage fatigue this week

My anxious thoughts are

Something I will do just for me this week

What's causing my anxiety?

I will schedule fun this week by

WEEK 36

Reflections

One thing that challenged me this week

What I learned from the challenge

A thought I need to let go of is

I will practice doing this by

I was proud of myself this week for

A moment at work that connected me back to my purpose was

How balanced did I feel this week (1-5)?

One balance tactic I'll do more next week

MONTHLY REFLECTION

What went well this month? What lessons did I apply from the focus journal that made me feel more balanced?

....

....

....

....

What was difficult? Where do I need to adjust either my physical goal or mental goal to be more balanced?

....

....

....

....

What is working well in my work environment? Do I need to adjust the way my shifts are scheduled? Is it time for me to schedule time off for the next month?

....

....

....

....

What would make me feel more supported and balanced at work? How could I suggest this change to my leadership team? My teammates?

....

....

....

....

How is my resilience growing? What experience did I bounce back from that made me proud?

....

....

....

....

One thing I will schedule just for me next month is

....

....

Learning from Challanges

Hardships can be learning opportunities and perhaps make us stronger once we emerge from the other side. Write about something that was difficult when it happened but was beneficial in the lesson you learned.

....
....
....
....
....
....
....
....
....
....
....
....
....
....
....
....
....
....
....
....
....
....
....
....
....
....
....

WEEK 37

Planning

I will care for myself at work this week by

My physical goal focus for this week

One way I will manage fatigue this week

My emotional goal focus for this week

Something I will do just for me this week

My anxious thoughts are

I will schedule fun this week by

What's causing my anxiety?

WEEK 37

Reflections

One thing that challenged me this week

What I learned from the challenge

A thought I need to let go of is

I will practice doing this by

I was proud of myself this week for

A moment at work that connected me back to my purpose was

How balanced did I feel this week (1-5)?

One balance tactic I'll do more next week

WEEK 38

Planning

I will care for myself at work this week by

My physical goal focus for this week

One way I will manage fatigue this week

My emotional goal focus for this week

Something I will do just for me this week

My anxious thoughts are

I will schedule fun this week by

What's causing my anxiety?

WEEK 38

Reflections

One thing that challenged me this week

What I learned from the challenge

A thought I need to let go of is

I will practice doing this by

I was proud of myself this week for

A moment at work that connected me back to my purpose was

How balanced did I feel this week (1-5)?

One balance tactic I'll do more next week

WEEK 39

Planning

I will care for myself at work this week by

My physical goal focus for this week

One way I will manage fatigue this week

My emotional goal focus for this week

Something I will do just for me this week

My anxious thoughts are

I will schedule fun this week by

What's causing my anxiety?

WEEK 39

Reflections

One thing that challenged me this week

What I learned from the challenge

A thought I need to let go of is

I will practice doing this by

I was proud of myself this week for

A moment at work that connected me back to my purpose was

How balanced did I feel this week (1-5)?

One balance tactic I'll do more next week

WEEK 40

Planning

I will care for myself at work this week by

My physical goal focus for this week

One way I will manage fatigue this week

My emotional goal focus for this week

Something I will do just for me this week

My anxious thoughts are

I will schedule fun this week by

What's causing my anxiety?

WEEK 40

Reflections

One thing that challenged me this week

What I learned from the challenge

A thought I need to let go of is

I will practice doing this by

I was proud of myself this week for

A moment at work that connected me back to my purpose was

How balanced did I feel this week (1-5)?

One balance tactic I'll do more next week

MONTHLY REFLECTION

What went well this month? What lessons did I apply from the focus journal that made me feel more balanced?

....

....

....

....

What was difficult? Where do I need to adjust either my physical goal or mental goal to be more balanced?

....

....

....

....

What is working well in my work environment? Do I need to adjust the way my shifts are scheduled? Is it time for me to schedule time off for the next month?

....

....

....

....

What would make me feel more supported and balanced at work? How could I suggest this change to my leadership team? My teammates?

....

....

....

....

How is my resilience growing? What experience did I bounce back from that made me proud?

....

....

....

One thing I will schedule just for me next month is

....

....

Focusing on Gratitude

What aspects of your role as a nurse are you grateful for? Reflect on a recent experience where you were flooded with feelings of gratitude for your opportunity to care for a patient.

....
....
....
....
....
....
....
....
....
....
....
....
....
....
....
....
....
....
....
....
....
....
....
....
....
....
....
....
....

WEEK 41

Planning

My physical goal focus for this week

I will care for myself at work this week by

My emotional goal focus for this week

One way I will manage fatigue this week

My anxious thoughts are

Something I will do just for me this week

What's causing my anxiety?

I will schedule fun this week by

WEEK 41

Reflections

One thing that challenged me this week

What I learned from the challenge

A thought I need to let go of is

I will practice doing this by

I was proud of myself this week for

A moment at work that connected me back to my purpose was

How balanced did I feel this week (1-5)?

One balance tactic I'll do more next week

WEEK 42

Planning

My physical goal focus for this week

I will care for myself at work this week by

My emotional goal focus for this week

One way I will manage fatigue this week

My anxious thoughts are

Something I will do just for me this week

What's causing my anxiety?

I will schedule fun this week by

WEEK 42

Reflections

One thing that challenged me this week

What I learned from the challenge

A thought I need to let go of is

I will practice doing this by

I was proud of myself this week for

A moment at work that connected me back to my purpose was

How balanced did I feel this week (1-5)?

One balance tactic I'll do more next week

WEEK 43

Planning

My physical goal focus for this week

I will care for myself at work this week by

My emotional goal focus for this week

One way I will manage fatigue this week

My anxious thoughts are

Something I will do just for me this week

What's causing my anxiety?

I will schedule fun this week by

WEEK 43

Reflections

One thing that challenged me this week

What I learned from the challenge

A thought I need to let go of is

I will practice doing this by

I was proud of myself this week for

A moment at work that connected me back to my purpose was

How balanced did I feel this week (1-5)?

One balance tactic I'll do more next week

WEEK 44

Planning

My physical goal focus for this week

I will care for myself at work this week by

My emotional goal focus for this week

One way I will manage fatigue this week

My anxious thoughts are

Something I will do just for me this week

What's causing my anxiety?

I will schedule fun this week by

WEEK 44

Reflections

One thing that challenged me this week

What I learned from the challenge

A thought I need to let go of is

I will practice doing this by

I was proud of myself this week for

A moment at work that connected me back to my purpose was

How balanced did I feel this week (1-5)?

One balance tactic I'll do more next week

MONTHLY REFLECTION

What went well this month? What lessons did I apply from the focus journal that made me feel more balanced?

....
....
....
....

What was difficult? Where do I need to adjust either my physical goal or mental goal to be more balanced?

....
....
....
....

What is working well in my work environment? Do I need to adjust the way my shifts are scheduled? Is it time for me to schedule time off for the next month?

....
....
....
....

What would make me feel more supported and balanced at work? How could I suggest this change to my leadership team? My teammates?

....
....
....
....

How is my resilience growing? What experience did I bounce back from that made me proud?

....
....
....
....

One thing I will schedule just for me next month is

....
....

Making Those Appointments

What wellness exams, preventative medicine or checkups have you missed in the last year? What needs to be scheduled now? Primary Checkup? Cancer screening? Dental care? Therapy? Eyes or Ear evaluation?

....

....

....

....

....

....

....

....

....

....

....

....

....

....

....

....

....

....

....

....

....

....

....

....

....

....

WEEK 45

Planning

I will care for myself at work this week by

My physical goal focus for this week

One way I will manage fatigue this week

My emotional goal focus for this week

Something I will do just for me this week

My anxious thoughts are

I will schedule fun this week by

What's causing my anxiety?

WEEK 45

Reflections

One thing that challenged me this week

What I learned from the challenge

A thought I need to let go of is

I will practice doing this by

I was proud of myself this week for

A moment at work that connected me back to my purpose was

How balanced did I feel this week (1-5)?

One balance tactic I'll do more next week

WEEK 46

Planning

I will care for myself at work this week by

My physical goal focus for this week

One way I will manage fatigue this week

My emotional goal focus for this week

Something I will do just for me this week

My anxious thoughts are

I will schedule fun this week by

What's causing my anxiety?

WEEK 46

Reflections

One thing that challenged me this week

What I learned from the challenge

A thought I need to let go of is

I will practice doing this by

I was proud of myself this week for

A moment at work that connected me back to my purpose was

How balanced did I feel this week (1-5)?

One balance tactic I'll do more next week

WEEK 47

Planning

My physical goal focus for this week

I will care for myself at work this week by

My emotional goal focus for this week

One way I will manage fatigue this week

My anxious thoughts are

Something I will do just for me this week

What's causing my anxiety?

I will schedule fun this week by

WEEK 47

Reflections

One thing that challenged me this week

What I learned from the challenge

A thought I need to let go of is

I will practice doing this by

I was proud of myself this week for

A moment at work that connected me back to my purpose was

How balanced did I feel this week (1-5)?

One balance tactic I'll do more next week

WEEK 48

Planning

My physical goal focus for this week

My emotional goal focus for this week

My anxious thoughts are

What's causing my anxiety?

I will care for myself at work this week by

One way I will manage fatigue this week

Something I will do just for me this week

I will schedule fun this week by

WEEK 48

Reflections

One thing that challenged me this week

What I learned from the challenge

A thought I need to let go of is

I will practice doing this by

I was proud of myself this week for

A moment at work that connected me back to my purpose was

How balanced did I feel this week (1-5)?

One balance tactic I'll do more next week

MONTHLY REFLECTION

What went well this month? What lessons did I apply from the focus journal that made me feel more balanced?

....
....
....
....

What was difficult? Where do I need to adjust either my physical goal or mental goal to be more balanced?

....
....
....
....

What is working well in my work environment? Do I need to adjust the way my shifts are scheduled? Is it time for me to schedule time off for the next month?

....
....
....
....

What would make me feel more supported and balanced at work? How could I suggest this change to my leadership team? My teammates?

....
....
....
....

How is my resilience growing? What experience did I bounce back from that made me proud?

....
....
....
....

One thing I will schedule just for me next month is

....
....

That Special Patient

Share about a special patient you will always remember. How have they impacted you for the better and have made you the nurse that you are today?

....
....
....
....
....
....
....
....
....
....
....
....
....
....
....
....
....
....
....
....
....
....
....
....
....
....
....

WEEK 49

Planning

My physical goal focus for this week

My emotional goal focus for this week

My anxious thoughts are

What's causing my anxiety?

I will care for myself at work this week by

One way I will manage fatigue this week

Something I will do just for me this week

I will schedule fun this week by

WEEK 49

Reflections

One thing that challenged me this week

What I learned from the challenge

A thought I need to let go of is

I will practice doing this by

I was proud of myself this week for

A moment at work that connected me back to my purpose was

How balanced did I feel this week (1-5)?

One balance tactic I'll do more next week

WEEK 50

Planning

My physical goal focus for this week

I will care for myself at work this week by

My emotional goal focus for this week

One way I will manage fatigue this week

My anxious thoughts are

Something I will do just for me this week

What's causing my anxiety?

I will schedule fun this week by

Reflections

One thing that challenged me this week

What I learned from the challenge

A thought I need to let go of is

I will practice doing this by

I was proud of myself this week for

A moment at work that connected me back to my purpose was

How balanced did I feel this week (1-5)?

One balance tactic I'll do more next week

WEEK 51

Planning

My physical goal focus for this week

I will care for myself at work this week by

My emotional goal focus for this week

One way I will manage fatigue this week

My anxious thoughts are

Something I will do just for me this week

What's causing my anxiety?

I will schedule fun this week by

WEEK 51

Reflections

One thing that challenged me this week

What I learned from the challenge

A thought I need to let go of is

I will practice doing this by

I was proud of myself this week for

A moment at work that connected me back to my purpose was

How balanced did I feel this week (1-5)?

One balance tactic I'll do more next week

WEEK 52

Planning

My physical goal focus for this week

I will care for myself at work this week by

My emotional goal focus for this week

One way I will manage fatigue this week

My anxious thoughts are

Something I will do just for me this week

What's causing my anxiety?

I will schedule fun this week by

WEEK 52

Reflections

One thing that challenged me this week

What I learned from the challenge

A thought I need to let go of is

I will practice doing this by

I was proud of myself this week for

A moment at work that connected me back to my purpose was

How balanced did I feel this week (1-5)?

One balance tactic I'll do more next week

End of Year Reflections

Review your journalings for the year, starting from week one. Take time to see your thought process evolution, how your goal focus changed, and what course corrections you made when you were unbalanced.

What new habits resulted from this process that have created more balance for you?

....
....
....
....
....
....
....

Resiliency is like a muscle. How has yours grown?

....
....
....
....
....
....
....

How has the focus journal work impacted your practice in patient care?

....
....
....
....
....
....
....
....
....
....

How have you grown in your personal life, aside from work?

....
....
....
....
....
....
....

Share a patient story that occurred this year that connects you back to why you became a nurse in the first place.

....
....
....
....
....
....
....
....
....
....
....
....
....
....
....
....
....

Notes